Albert Whitehouse
Home Brewing
an illustrated guide

DAVID & CHARLES
Newton Abbot   London   North Pomfret (Vt)

With sincere thanks to my wife, Gwen,
for the use of her kitchen
and her help with the photographs
and to Frank Chapman who developed the films
and made the enlargements

British Library Cataloguing in Publication Data

Whitehouse, Albert
  Home brewing
  1. Brewing—Amateur's manuals
  I. Title
  641.8'73   TP570

  ISBN 0-7153-7985-2

© Albert Whitehouse 1981

First published 1981
Second impression 1982

Printed in Great Britain
by Redwood Burn Ltd Trowbridge Wilts.
for David & Charles (Publishers) Limited
Brunel House Newton Abbot Devon

Published in the United States of America
by David & Charles Inc
North Pomfret Vermont 05053 USA

Contents

Introduction

No one knows for certain when or where the fermentation process was discovered. The ancient Egyptians were brewing beer 5,000 years ago and there is no reason to suppose that they were the first.

In prehistoric times people must have realised that any liquid mixed with vegetable or fruit substances goes sour if kept for any length of time, particularly if left in an open container. At some time in the distant past the discovery was made that under certain conditions this liquid would not go 'off' but actually improve—and so alcohol was made.

Having achieved this remarkable result once they must have set about trying to repeat the process and we now know that they were successful. As time went by other people learned about it and made their own drinks in their own way. When fruit or vegetables from which to make their drinks were unavailable, they discovered that grain could be used instead.

From then on, those who were better at brewing than others sold their surplus. As time went by, their descendants became influential, very rich and well known by the name of their brew. However, laws were introduced which discouraged home brewing.

In 1963 the law was changed and home brewing again became popular. By making it themselves, beer drinking enthusiasts found they could produce a very acceptable alcoholic drink at a much lower price than that on sale to the general public as it was not taxed. Today very much more is known about barley, malt, yeast and hops, and the equipment available has greatly improved, making the whole process very much easier.

Brewing can be very conveniently divided into nine stages, each requiring widely differing degrees of knowledge and skill:

1 GROWING hops and cereals and other crops which will produce sugar
2 MILLING and crushing grain
3 MALTING barley and producing concentrates in powder or syrup form
4 MASHING the barley and other cereals to produce wort by infusion or decoction
5 STERILISING and STABILISING the wort by boiling and adding hops
6 FERMENTATION to change the sugar into alcohol
7 BOTTLING and cask filling
8 STORAGE and transportation
9 SERVING and sampling the end product and deciding whether to follow exactly the same method again or to make modifications

Growing cereals and hops is a job for the farmer. Milling, crushing and malting are beyond the scope of the home brewer as the average home does not possess the necessary facilities. It is convenient, therefore, to start home brewing with a variation of stage 4.

The brewer's role

If you are a man, it can be a good idea to try to produce a brew which the ladies enjoy drinking. Once you have produced a beer, a lager, or a stout which the ladies find acceptable, you are likely to have more co-operation from your 'satisfied customers', but if you keep on producing beer which they do not like even though you think it is fine, there may not be much future for you in your home brewing. It is a home activity and the family, your relations, and your friends will expect to enjoy the end product.

If you are a woman brewer—well, the kitchen is your domain so there is no need to worry!

If you produce an unacceptable drink which is too bitter, too dry, too cloudy, do not despair; it happens, even in the best of breweries. No one can sit at a desk and devise a precise recipe and method so take heart—successful home brewing is achieved by trial, error and experiment and is based largely upon previous experience.

The opportunities to experiment are endless, but first brew an acceptable drink which you can use as a norm. Record the recipe and method in detail for your next brew.

What is in a name?

Beer, lager, and stout are the names given to three alcoholic drinks based on malt, hops, water and yeast, but brewed with very important different treatments at critical stages to produce varying flavour, colour, 'fullness' and level of alcohol. Unless there is a specific reference to home brewed lager and stout in the following pages, it can be assumed that what applies to beer also applies to them.

Types of malt

Of the five cereals—barley, wheat, oats, maize and rice—home brewing mostly relies on barley which produces the best malt and flavour. Twelve different packs of malt grain and extract are shown in the picture.

Barley is a hardy crop. Experts employed by commercial brewers inspect it from the early days of its growth and buy it whilst it is growing. They know what type of barley they require for brews planned more than a year ahead. It varies from county to county and throughout the world.

What home brewers buy is not even a named

variety. No home brewer can produce a drink the same as a famous commercial brew. Home-brewed beer is different stuff completely; some say it is as good, some say it is better. Nobody readily admits to it being worse!

Production of malt has become a specialist industry and to sprout grain and roast it success-fully to pale crystal malt, medium, or dark malt is beyond the competence of the average brewer in his kitchen at home.

There are many sorts of barley and barley malt available from High Street stores, chemists and brewing suppliers: plain or ground barley grain; crystal malt, pale to dark, whole or crushed; malt extract in powder form, pale, medium, or dark; malt extract in syrup form in tins or jars, light or dark; torrified barley. All these are illustrated on page 5.

Other cereals

Some wheat may be used for special brews; oats may be required for stout; maize gives a flavour and improves beer by adding 'body'.

Cereals illustrated on the left show: (left to right, top row) dark crushed malt, pale malt grain, whole dark crystal malt, ground pale crystal malt; (left to right, bottom row) torrified barley, crushed oats, whole crystal malt, flaked maize.

Flaked maize is a useful adjunct which seems to add a piquant flavour and body. Use a small amount and increase it gradually by experiment.

Flaked oats are worth trying in dark beers but are not highly recommended.

Torrified barley is produced like pop-corn and reputed to give beer a nutty flavour and good head retention. It lives up to its reputation and is best used in small quantities.

Strainers

Unless you use a kit with the wort supplied in a can as syrup which only requires the addition of hot water, you cannot make beer without having to use some sort of strainer.

A plastic model is useful for a start, but not very strong, and a metal strainer is preferable. The largest domestic strainers hold 1kg (2·2lb) of grain.

A nylon bag is highly recommended for 10 litre (2 gallon) work (see illustration on page 11 of crystal malt in a nylon bag being crushed). A nylon bag with the stitching picked away is useful as a covering in conjunction with a strainer over a large fermenting bin and one in use is shown on page 24. Nylon bags are available in three sizes of mesh and can be used many times. Cotton sleeves which can be tied as a bag are available but can only be used once. Grains in some kits are supplied in disposable cotton bags.

Storage space

Some equipment and ingredients partly used or unopened and held in readiness for the next brew on a shelf. Even brewing on a modest scale will require a reasonable amount of drawer, shelf or cupboard space.

With the shortage of storage space in many homes today the amount of space which can be devoted to brewing activities might be a deciding factor in the output. A new convert should seriously consider what space is available before making a start.

Considering how and where to store the end product before beginning the brewing may appear backwards thinking, but in actual fact it is very sound. A small 10 litre (2 gallon) container and a few bottles is a good quantity to start with. There is less to lose if it goes wrong and if it is just about drinkable there is less of it to be disposed of and you can get on with the next brew more quickly. That you will progress to 25 litre (5½ gallon) brewing is almost certain, once you have the experience and provided you have the space.

Ultimately you will buy your ingredients to keep at least one or two brews in hand and you will always have things to store. A drawer is more convenient than a shelf for ingredients; save the shelf for bottles full of beer and the hardware.

Weighing grain

Without a pair of scales a home brewer must work at a disadvantage. The scales in the picture, shown weighing 800g (1lb 14oz) of grain, are balanced and will weigh very small quantities. Most domestic scales are calibrated to weigh in small units of 25g or 1oz and these are useful, but those which are calibrated in 50g or 2oz are adequate. Any lighter weights can be measured by spoon—one ounce either way will not make too much difference and that is roughly two heaped tablespoons.

Brewing log

To be successful the home brewer must keep a log of all the ingredients, times, temperatures, amounts of hot and cold water, type of yeast used, and notes on taste and flavour, clearing times and keeping qualities. Without it a recipe cannot be repeated or improved by modifying the amount or changes in the type or supply of ingredients, as may be required to improve it on the next occasion. Any brewer worthy of the name will continuously seek for improvements. Only when a favourite brew can be repeated from memory because it is so good, will the log become superfluous.

Washing grain

The picture shows grain being washed in a strainer, an optional process undertaken after finding that some grain, although it looked and smelled all right, produced an 'earthy' taste in the brew. It took a long time to trace the fault but after washing more from the same batch the next brew was very much improved. It is a choice the brewer has to make after inspecting the grain. It does no harm to try it washed and unwashed, including whole crystal malt. Obviously you cannot wash crushed or milled grain.

Mashing barley

Beer was being brewed before sugar became important and replaced honey as a sweetener. Mashing barley produces sugar; and the more efficient the mash, the more sugar produced. It also produces flavour.

In home brewing you can forego some of the sugar production in mashing by adding the real thing separately, and concentrate your efforts on obtaining flavour which is produced by the action of water and heat on grain and hops in the saucepan over a controlled period of time.

Professional brewers produce wort which naturally contains sugar and then boil it with hops in two separate steps, but home brewers can boil grain and hops in one operation to get the flavour and add sugar and barley malt extract in order to obtain the wort. It is a more expensive and less efficient process for the home brewer but it works.

Saucepans—how big?

The illustration shows two domestic saucepans and a preserving pan of 2pt, 6pt and 16pt capacity respectively.

The small saucepan can be used but is really not big enough for serious home brewing. The medium size is satisfactory for 10 and 25 litre brewing. The large preserving pan can be used but it imposes limitations because of its weight when full of liquid.

Before buying a saucepan especially for home brewing, the brewer should thoroughly clean and try out whatever may be available in the home and evaluate its potential, and then decide what size will be most suitable.

Preparing a mash for infusion

One of the methods used by the pioneers of home brewing was to infuse a mash in the oven and here the mash is being prepared. Every convert should know how this method works as an aid to understanding the easy way. It is not suggested that this is the best way.

The method is known as infusion and not to be confused with another method known as decoction. With the infusion method which is used commercially to produce wort, grains known as 'grist' are brought together in a mash tun and stirred with hot water for a number of hours. The temperature is critical.

In decoction, which is more complicated, the mash starts at a lower temperature and periodically some of the liquid is drawn off and boiled and then returned to the tun to raise the temperature. Over decades of experience professional brewers have found the optimum size of grist which suits them best, so the grain is mixed and milled to their house requirements.

Using milled or crushed grain can raise problems for the home brewer with sparging which is the next operation, so the grains here are left whole and mixed with 2oz flaked maize and added to the water which is at a temperature of 65°C ready to be placed in the oven which is at that same temperature.

Anyone with a solid fuel cooker such as an Aga can prepare a mash and leave it in a warm oven overnight, with very good results.

Instead of using an oven to carry out an infusion is possible to do it in an insulated box in which you place the grain and water at a slightly higher temperature than you require and allow it to fall to a lower temperature over a period of time, usually overnight. You would have to make the box yourself and it is not an easy job.

Stainless steel and plastic boilers are available with a capacity of up to 25 litres (5½ gallons) which is about the maximum realistic quantity for a home brew. These boilers are fitted with a detachable strainer and a tap so that wort can be drawn off. The grains are removed and the hot wort is returned to the boiler to be brought to boiling point and held at that temperature for an hour with the hops or as long as the recipe requires.

The difficulty facing the ordinary man or woman in the kitchen at home is having space for moving five gallons of hot liquid in and out of such a boiler to be used exclusively for brewing.

Infusion in progress

Grains in water at 65°C (149°F). The stainless steel bowl used here happened to be the largest and most convenient container to hand. Any other large bowl will do providing it will go into the oven easily and you can get it out at the end of two hours when it will be very hot to handle.

If a thermometer is available use it to check the temperature but otherwise you can rely on the oven setting; modern ovens have thermostatic controls which are very accurate.

During infusion, malted barley releases starch, maltose and dextrine, and other constituent parts of the grain most readily when it is soaking in a temperature between 60°C and 68°C (140°F and 155°F). It should be stirred occasionally. The liquid produced becomes the wort which is fermented into beer.

The mash has to be kept at its temperature for a good period of time; heat and time are two factors which help to determine the quality of the wort. It is much too difficult and complicated a method for the result achieved when more simple alternatives are available which give equally good results.

Crystal malt

Some people hold the view that if crystal malt is used whole the full flavour is not brought out, and that it should be crushed or milled before use. Others claim that just breaking the husk with a rolling pin is sufficient. A third group, including

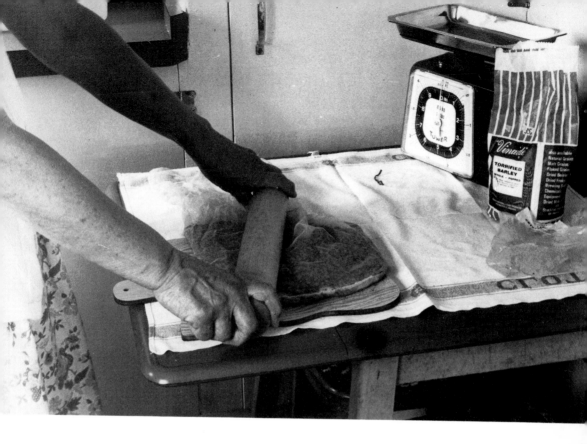

purveyors of brewing kits, virtually say use it whole because they pack it that way, and you thus save yourself a straining problem.

The illustration shows crystal malt in a nylon bag being cracked with a rolling pin. In this method the malt is placed in the bag first and is cracked before the hops and other grains are added. The bag is then tied up to prevent spillage during boiling.

Crystal malt gives the brew a good flavour; pale is used for lager, light ale, and bitter; amber for mild; dark, black, and patent malt for stout.

Combinations of light and dark malt in varying quantities give a wide range of flavours and colours.

Hops

Weighing hops is not the easiest of tasks if you want to be really accurate, but accuracy is not so very important—a few hops either way in your brews will not make that much difference. One uff and bits float away like baby moths.

Normally packets on sale weigh 4oz, 6oz or 8oz; sometimes in pounds. Unless you have a lot of brewing on hand it is best to buy a small quantity

and use them all rather than keeping a stock a
their quality deteriorates if not kept properly.

It is a good sign if the hops are springy. Hop
which are dry and lifeless are suspect.

The amount used naturally depends upon th
type of brew; ½oz per gallon is considered 'light'
2oz per gallon 'heavy'.

Varieties most useful to the home brewer are:
Hallertau, Styrian Goldings, Saaz for light ale an
lager; Goldings, East Kent Goldings, Bramlin
Cross for pale ale and bitter; Fuggles, Norther
Brewer, for mild beer; Fuggles, Norther
Brewer, Bullion for strong beer and stout.

All hops can be blended in combination witl
each other so that special desirable feature
of each can be utilised to the full. A few experi
mental brews will prove the qualities of each.

The hop rate affects the bitterness—low ho₁
rate for lager to high hop rate for best bitter witl
the others somewhere in between.

Hops can be obtained in compressed form i₁
wrapped blocks of one pound in weight. Thes
have to be broken for use to get the weight righ
but they soon disintegrate in warm water. Hop
can also be bought in pellet form, as concentrate
essence or as a powder.

Using hops whole and dried served the trad
well for centuries and there does not seem to be an
reason for the home brewer to change. Without ex
perience with the real thing how can you te.
whether the essence or concentrate is better? Con
verting them to these other forms was probably t
serve economic pressures on time, carriage
storage, and handling. It is unlikely that it wa
principally done to improve the beer although a
improvement may have occurred arising fron
standardisation of the product and its keepin
qualities.

Adding the hops

'A handful is an ounce' is an old saying. If th
recipe requires some hops to be added towards th
end of a boiling you can take it that a handful is ad
equate.

In most recipes hops are added to the wo₁
before it is brought to the boil. Some can be save
and used at the end and some can be held back fc
what is called 'dry hopping' when some of the hop
are added to the barrel—a long tradition in th
trade. Dry hopping is not possible if the beer
being bottled.

The aromatic value and the various oils in hop
respond to different treatments very noticeably.

requires a long time in boiling water to extract all the substances, but in that way the aroma is lost. You have to endeavour to strike a good balance.

Originally added and boiled with the wort, hops were used for their sterilising, medicinal, antiseptic, and preservative qualities. Nowadays they are used for their bitterness, aroma and flavour.

The questions are when to add them; how much to add; which variety or what mixture of varieties? This is a broad area for experiment for you as a home brewer who can adjust the hops to suit your favourite brew.

Whilst being boiled, resins, acids and volatile substances are released and some of these help to clear the beer which is a very useful additional attribute. At first the home brewer may find a degree of confusion with the wide choice being offered and not be able to detect the merits of the different varieties. That phase passes and after a short time the merits of each become clear and you will find an improvement in your beer!

A minimum boiling of half an hour is desirable but there is nothing to prevent an experiment with older recipes which required a roll for two hours.

Water

Water is the main constituent of beer, the others being alcohol, colouring and flavour. In home brewing you have to manage with what comes out of the tap; it can be 'hardened' or 'softened' to some degree, but your treatment of it might be inconsistent and in that respect your beer will be affected by the water.

An analysis can be obtained from your Area Water Authority free of charge but might show different values for boreholes in the same district; you cannot know exactly what you are getting unless you analyse it at the tap. So an analysis whilst being interesting is not all that helpful.

'Soft' water is recommended for making stout and lager; 'hard' water is considered to be good for producing bitter beer. Rain water is not suitable for brewing, mainly because of the impurities collected in it as it falls or from dust on the roof down which it runs.

It is hardly worth the trouble of altering the water which is readily available to you so accept what comes out of your tap or from your pump, if you happen to have a well. Until you have some experience with that you cannot know what changes you would want to make anyway to improve your beer. It might even be so good that you will not wish to change it.

When you have enough experience and feel you ought to try modifying the water by adding gypsum (calcium sulphate) epsom salt (magnesium sulphate) or salt (sodium chloride) to harden it, you should obtain an analysis from your Area Authority and ask their assistance. They can be very helpful in suggesting an answer to your problem. Ultimately you might decide that it was all not worthwhile and just stick to tap or well water in future.

The more you go into the subject the more complicated and technical it becomes. After all, you don't go to all that trouble over beverages like tea, coffee, or cocoa, so why bother about your home brewed beer, which in terms of cost on a pint for pint basis is about equal.

Malt extract

Pouring 1kg (2·2lb) malt extract into a preserving pan with hops and grain in preparation for boiling to make a 25 litre brew.

This pan contained 1lb crystal malt, ¼lb flaked maize, 2oz torrified barley, ½lb glucose chips, 3oz Bramling Cross hops, and was brought to boil and allowed to roll for half an hour, when a handful of hops was added and stirred in. After a further twenty minutes it was poured through a strainer into a 25 litre (5½ gallon) fermenting bin onto sugar which had been dissolved with boiling water.

Colour

Caramel in the form of gravy browning can be added to obtain an amber colouring in a brew using light malt. One teaspoon is sufficient, but you learn by experience if you prefer more. It should be added to the wort before boiling and has no noticeable affect upon the flavour.

There are alternatives for achieving a similar result. Dark crystal malt with the grain has the added advantage that it can also affect the flavour by adding a dryness or a tang if that is what you want. Dark powdered malt extract added in this way has the affect of producing a smoother drink. Dark brown sugar will also alter the colour.

If it is only the colour you are concerned with, gravy browning (which is caramel—burnt sugar, salt and glucose syrup) is probably easiest and best but be sure that the one you use has not been flavoured by the addition of spices.

Stirring and rolling the brew

Stirring in all the ingredients in a preserving pan. If you are aiming for a light ale or a lager-type beer, you can start the operation with cold water and very slowly bring the temperature to 66–71°C (150–160°F) and hold it around that heat by switching off. 10 litres (2 gallons) of hot water will hold its temperature on an electric hot plate for some time; when it falls, after about ten minutes, you switch on again to regain the necessary heat. You may have to switch on and off several times in an hour. A gas stove demands a different technique.

Alternatively, start with hot water about 71°C (160°F) and put in the ingredients which will lower the temperature and then continue with the occasional switch on and off.

Yet another method is to start from cold with all the ingredients added and let it come right up to the boil on a very low heat which may take an hour or more depending on how low you can get the heat at the start, your cooker and the size of saucepan, dixie or preserving pan.

Having reached boiling point you then let it roll for not less than half an hour.

Each of these methods can affect the flavour of your beer and also its clarity; if you go on too long minute substances which boiling brings into suspension can cause a haze which might affect the appearance though not the taste.

The second picture illustrates the wort rolling and shows how much water has been lost through evaporation. You can make good this loss immediately with hot water, or with cold water in the fermentation bin which is preferable because there is less weight of hot liquid to handle when pouring.

Using a 6pt saucepan

Light crystal malt, torrified barley, flaked maize and hops mixed together in a medium to large size saucepan for a 25 litre brew.

Stir from time to time to prevent the mixture sticking.

Leaving off the saucepan lid helps to keep down the temperature or prolong the time taken to raise it. Putting on the lid helps to retain the temperature if you apply the switching technique described previously.

An option with a 6pt saucepan is to start at 66°C (150°F) and quickly reach boiling point,

then drain off from the mash, followed by a further boil again starting at 66°C by taking hot water from a kettle.

Additional water has to be added to the fermentation bin when you use a small saucepan. The 6pt size illustrated is not small by normal domestic standards only in the context of being used to brew 25 litres of beer.

Fermentation capacity

There are many sizes of fermentation vessels on the market ranging from 10 to 25 litre (2 to 5½ gallon) capacity and these two sizes are shown in the illustrations on the left.

At best, the small 10 litre size will provide one pint bottle of beer per day continuously. It takes one week for the beer to ferment and it takes one week standing to fall clear. The longer it stands in the bottle, the better it will be.

The system gives you a margin of fourteen days in which to make a new brew to go into the bottles when they become empty. You cannot shorten this period successfully and have naturally matured beer.

The larger fermentation container works in conjunction with more bottles or a barrel and that, in turn, is determined by your storage space. It will still take the same time for the beer to clear in the bottle, but it will be standing longer and you will brew less often. Beer takes longer to mature in a barrel.

Crock, glass and china fermentation vessels are prone to breakage and not very satisfactory. Crock vessels in particular have problems when the glaze becomes cracked. The only metal which is satisfactory is stainless steel. Purpose-made plastic containers are available which are thoroughly reliable and safe to use.

Sterilisation and hygiene

Fermentation bins can be partly sterilised before use by boiling water poured direct from the kettle; this helps to avoid infestation of the wort by wild yeast or other undesirable organisms.

Cleanliness is essential. The absolute minimum requirement is to wash down the containers with cold water before use but even this may not be sufficient unless a sterilising solution is used.

A good steriliser is a mixture of sodium metabisulphate and citric acid, both being soluble in water and easy to rinse away. One teaspoonful of each in a half litre of water is a powerful sterilisation agent, and should not be confused with a cleansing agent which you might use for glass bottles.

Sugar

Adding 500g sugar to a small brew (above).

Sugar is a prime component and it is fairly safe to assume that sugar straight from the bag is clean and carries no undesirable organism likely to affect the beer, so that it can be scalded and liquefied straight away. If in doubt it should be boiled.

There is not much difference between white imported and white home-grown sugar, but there is a noticeable difference between demerara and any white. Soft brown sugar does not have the same constituents as demerara but is very useful in dark beers.

Treacle, syrup and glucose chips give body but are not very suitable for light beers. Honey is worth at least one experiment but should be boiled because of likely contamination from wild yeasts. Invert sugar saves time, but the time saved may not be worth the extra trouble of inverting it yourself or its extra cost. Glucose chips are useful for adding 'body' as well as sugar.

Lactose and saccharine

A slightly sweet drink cannot be achieved by using sugar because it changes to alcohol during fermentation. Sweetness can be introduced by adding a very small quantity of good quality lactose or one or two saccharine tablets to the wort before boiling.

Use of glucose chips

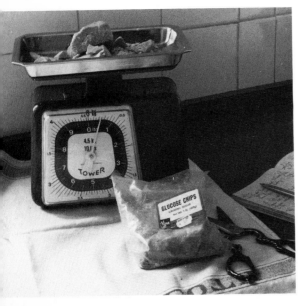

Weighing out 225g (8oz) of glucose chips for a 10 litre brew and adding the chips to a saucepan for boiling with hops and grain.

Glucose chips are ideal for brewing and, whilst more expensive than sugar, are considered to be worth the extra cost. A trial brew with glucose chips will establish their merits for noting in the log. They can be blended with other sugars but always have to be boiled.

Dry powdered malt extract

Malt in powdered form is the home brewer's gift from the trade. It can be measured more easily than the malt syrup extract, and if you do not need the full packet there is no problem in storing the remainder until you can use it.

Available in light and dark forms, there is very considerable difference between brands—particularly the dark varieties where some brands are much lighter than others.

The home brewer can achieve numerous satisfactory results with a blend of dry malts, from a fine lager-type brew with all light malt to a stout type with all dark.

The quantity of malt to be added should not be less than one pound per gallon when used on its own, but when sugar and the hot water with extracts from boiling grain are added, this can be reduced. Sugar and dried malt should be taken as one for the purpose of calculating the amount of sugar in the gallon.

It can be boiled with the grain and hops or treated separately and scalded with boiling water in the fermentation bin.

Two pounds of dried malt boiled for half an hour with suitable hops will produce 10 litres (2 gallons) of a very light lager-type drink; from this beginning you can increase the malt and hops, add sugar, glucose chips, crystal malt, flaked maize and dark malt which, together with a more potent hop, will produce a stronger drink like a mild or pale ale.

Malt syrup extract

Pouring dark malt syrup extract into a 25 litre fermentation bin prior to scalding.

Malt syrup extract is available in light and dark forms and has a distinctive characteristic in the finished beer. Available in jars and cans, it can be poured more easily if it is stood in a basin of hot water beforehand although that soaks off the label. Swill out the jar or can to obtain all the malt.

The scalding referred to above is a short cut and an exercisable option for the home brewer who should try both methods; the other is described on page 14 when the malt is boiled with the grain and hops.

It is safe to assume that malt extract will be sterile having been produced from a wort from which the water has been evaporated. Scalding with hot or boiling water should, therefore, be adequate. If the manufacturer says so or if you are in doubt, boil it to be sure of a completely sterile wort.

Adding powdered dark malt

Adding a dessertspoon of dark powdered malt to a 10 litre fermentation bin prior to scalding with hot or boiling water.

Unless you are attempting a stout-type brew when all dark malt will be required, a bag of dark powdered malt is useful to have around purely for adding to light malt to produce a more acceptable amber colour in the brew. It also adds a strong, smoother flavour.

An all-powdered light-malt-type brew may appear insipid but this can be overcome by adding a small quantity of dark malt, the amount to suit you being determined by trial and error and a record kept for reference. One whole heaped dessertspoon, say half an ounce, is enough for a trial brew and can be increased as experience is gained.

This method of colouring a brew is superior to the method on page 14 because you can be certain of also adding flavour.

Alcohol

The amount of alcohol in your finished beer will be determined by the amount of sugar in the wort before the yeast is pitched. Additional sugar can be added as fermentation progresses.

A good medium beer will have 4–5% alcohol; below that the keeping quality is not very good. A lager or light ale has about 4% alcohol, and a stout or strong ale about 6%. Over that you start producing 'Old Ale' or barley wine. Although beer with a high alcohol content will keep for months, it might prove too strong to drink in normal quantities.

The scale on a good hydrometer will show that to obtain 1% alcohol you need about 6oz of sugar for 2 gallons (10 litres).

Flavour

Flavour is the most important aspect of any brew. The flavour can be affected in many ways—you can vary the ingredients by choice and weight; you can vary the method of handling them; the temperatures to which they are subjected; the sustained times at different temperatures. Knowing how to do it successfully and then being able to repeat it again and again without any variation is perhaps the whole secret of brewing skill.

Additional requirements

One jar, one packet and three plastic containers hold all the extra items in addition to malt, hops, sugar and yeast which the home brewer requires.

Irish Moss is a seaweed (carragheen) with special properties and is added to the wort before it is boiled; isinglass finings are added to the beer after fermentation. Both these contribute to producing clear and bright beer. It is obvious that these must act in different ways to achieve a similar result. Of the two Irish Moss is the more uncertain and requires experience because it is used as a preventative measure, whereas with a finings you can see the extent of the problem before you use it. It is undoubtedly better to avoid

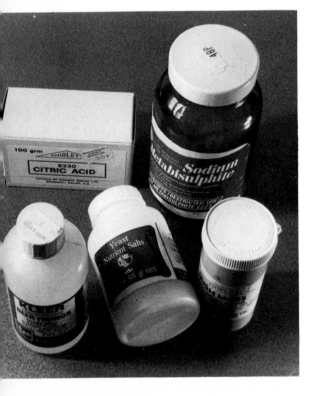

having to use either and with care they can be avoided.

Yeast nutrient containing ammonium sulphate, diammonium phosphate and magnesium sulphate supplements food in the brew should it be deficient for yeast requirements. Sodium metabisulphate is used for sterilising purposes and is a substance permitted by law in the food and drink trade. In combination with citric acid its fumes will indicate how powerful it is.

Nutrients

A small 2g spoonful of yeast nutrient being added as an insurance against slow fermentation. Citric acid can be used separately and it helps to sharpen the taste, but too much will spoil it.

Under normal circumstances barley malt has all the nutrients which yeast will require for it to perform its task of fermenting the sugar. The only nutrients you should require for brewing beer are all contained in a 100g bottle which will be enough to last a brewing season.

Always remember that these are micronutrients to be measured in parts per million. A spoonful of all four mixed together in a 10 litre brew is a hefty dose.

Preparation for 'sparging'

Pouring wort from the grains after infusion in the oven for two hours (see illustration on page 10. The aroma which arises is good and, if you decide to use this method, you will know that this is the right way to treat barley.

Wort produced this way is as near to the professional method as the home brewer can achieve in a small kitchen with only a stove on which to do the work. Some people think it worthwhile.

Gloves are necessary to protect hands because of the heat. The 1kg of grain used for this mash will produce 10 litres of 'thin' wort after 'sparging' which is the next stage.

It is an important part of this operation to maintain the temperature, so the strainer should be warmed before use.

All the hot grain is emptied into the strainer which in this case is standing inside another strainer to support it over a 10 litre plastic bucket, with a jug of hot water standing ready for use and the kettle boiling in case it is required.

Culinary equipment should be kept exclusively for brewing if possible as it otherwise has to be thoroughly cleaned before and after use.

'Sparging' the mash

Hot water being gently poured over the grains to extract all the flavour, sugar, nutrients and colour. The water and mash should be at the same temperature.

Grains are left whole for this method because of the difficulty of straining (see page 9). A mash of milled grain cannot be put into a strainer such as the one in the picture because the mesh is too coarse to hold back fine particles, but a finer mesh would become clogged. Using whole grain is a poor compromise for the real thing but it does give a tolerable result.

This method is cumbersome and time consuming and does not utilise all the grain's potential for making a good beer. The water should be hot and ideally used in the form of a very fine spray to cover the whole of the surface, but considerable ingenuity is required to arrange this. Water direct from the hot tap may not be satisfactory.

Wort produced this way has next to be boiled with hops to stabilise and sterilise it. In the process flavours are extracted and various substances from the grain and the hops are brought into suspension or coagulated and precipitated. It is known as the 'hot break'. The extent and vigour of the boil (roll) will affect the finished beer and the cost of fuel. Less than one hour boil may not be satisfactory.

Pouring and straining (1)

Pouring a very simple and easily-made brew of 10 litres (2 gallons). The ingredients in this brew were ½lb crystal malt crushed with a rolling pin and 2oz Northern Brewer hops put together in a nylon bag (see page 11) in 3½ litres (6 pints) water which was brought to the boil and then rolled for an hour.

There is no problem with straining; after the hot water has been poured, fresh cold water is run into the saucepan over the nylon bag to extract any remaining flavours in the hops and malt and is then added to the bucket to make it up to 10 litres.

Equal amounts of light powdered malt extract and sugar to make 1kg in weight are placed in the bucket and scalded with the hot wort.

Simple alternative methods using the same ingredients, saucepan and fermentation produce a different brew. For instance, if all the water is boiled by refilling the saucepan and bringing it to the boil, the brew will taste different because boiling takes minerals out of water. If half the hops are held back and introduced in the last fifteen minutes the flavour will be changed. Boiling the powdered malt with the other ingredients will also affect the flavour.

Half a teaspoon of yeast nutrient or citric acid or both added will not only ensure a good fermentation but will also affect the flavour—not adversely.

This size brew is ideal for experimentation. It is easy to handle and if the experiment is not highly successful and only a mediocre beer results, not a great deal has been lost but much experience gained. Remember the old saying 'there is no bad beer, some is just better than others'.

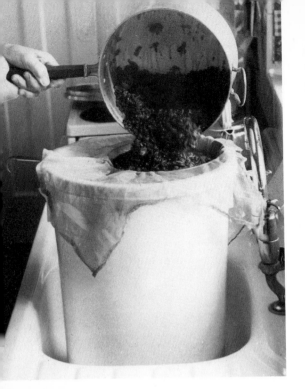

Pouring and straining (2)

Pouring and straining a 25 litre (5½ gallon) brew. This brew was made with 450g (1lb) crystal malt, 115g (4oz) flaked maize, 55g (2oz) torrified barley, 55g (2oz) Fuggles hops, brought to the boil and rolled for one hour, when a further 30g (1oz) of hops were added. It was poured onto 450g (1lb) of light powdered malt, 450g (1lb) of dark powdered malt, and 450g (1lb) white sugar and 450g (1lb) demerara sugar.

A metal strainer and unpicked nylon bag are being used for straining the mash which is then 'sparged' once with hot water direct from a kettle. Cold fresh water is then run through the mash to extract all the colour and flavour until the bin contains 25 litres. The mash for a 25 litre brew is too bulky for a nylon bag because the grain movement becomes restricted.

There are many variations for this method of brewing from light wort for a lager type to dark wort for a stout type of drink; each time you brew, keep a note of the details in case you want to repeat it. There is nothing worse than having a lovely drink which everybody likes and you have forgotten the recipe.

Pouring and straining (3)

A preserving pan in use for a 25 litre brew (opposite). All the ingredients are boiled together in this large vessel which has no lid but is designed to make pouring easy. Round or oval vessels of this capacity with lids usually have no facility to help pouring.

Pans of this size present a few problems for the home brewer because of the sheer weight involved when it comes to the straining operation. Unless you ladle out the water it has to be poured and two gallons of water plus the ingredients and the pan itself are not easy to move around, particularly when it is hot.

The best way is probably to bring the fermentation bin to the cooker and pour through a strainer direct into it. The bin can be raised on a strong box or low stool to a suitable height to prevent splashing.

Reverting to an earlier point about using a water boiler for the mash and 'sparging' it to collect 25

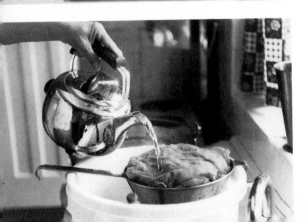

tres of wort, it should be made clear that with one
boiler of 25 litre capacity, the mash has to be
cleaned out and the wort transferred back to it for
boiling. It was because of the problems of transfer-
ing liquids that old breweries were not built all
one level, but later steam and then electric pumps
gave the brewer flexibility and he was able to move
liquids by pressure at will. The home brewer has
the same problem in a smaller way; 25 litres is a fair
weight and is just about the maximum quantity
that can be handled conveniently.

It is much easier to use a 6pt or 8pt capacity
saucepan on a cooker in a small kitchen for making
a 10 litre or larger brew and then gravitate to
bigger equipment with experience. There is no
need to envy those who have a small boiler and a
large kitchen in which to use it. Good beer has
been made in saucepans for a very long time and
will continue to be so made. You just have to do it
more often. The smaller brew also has the advantage of allowing you to experiment more often.

Rousing the brew

Stirring in all the ingredients before pitching
the yeast.

The old fashioned way of doing this was with a
long-handled wooden tool with a round base per-
forated with holes as wide as your thumb. It fitted
into a bucket so that it did not get contaminated by
being put down on the floor and could be scalded
before use. When pushed up and down and
pushed and pulled backwards and forwards, it
roused the brew by making the beer rush through
the holes until it was thoroughly stirred and
mixed.

Using a paddle to stir a large brew was less effective and much harder work, leading to spillage by
splashing. At home, a good clean wooden spoon is
effective in a 25 litre brew bin; plastic paddles tend
to bend. Scald it first or sterilise it in a solution. If
the brew is not roused, all the sugar will stay at the
bottom.

Taking the temperature of
the wort

A thermometer being used to ensure that the
wort is not too hot for the yeast (see page 29). The
10 litre bucket is standing in cold water to help it to
cool.

Wort is always vulnerable to contamination or

infection by wild yeasts, but never more so than i
this critical period whilst it is being coolec
Professional brewers have means of cooling th
wort when it is being transported through a totall
enclosed system to the fermentation bin, but th
home brewer has to rely on more primitiv
methods.

If the plastic holding the brew is warm to th
touch, it is too hot for the yeast.

Measuring the strength of the brew

Floating a hydrometer in the beer to chec
specific gravity (sg) before adding the yeast.

A hydrometer is essential. Without it yo
cannot know the sg and how much alcohol ther
will be after fermentation. Pure water bein
universally accepted as the norm, a hydromete
floated in it will show a figure of 1000 at
temperature of 59°F. Liquid with a sg lower tha
water will show a three-figure number such as 99
which indicates there is another substance lighte
than water in suspension in it, whereas a liqui
such as beer wort with a sg higher may read 1·034
In practice the decimal point is dropped and onl
the last two figures are shown on som
hydrometers.

Hydrometers are also shown on pages 28 an
33.

Sugar raises the sg and a home-brewin
hydrometer will measure the amount in a gallo
and show it on a scale; there is no other way t
measure the sugar content once it is dissolved i
the liquid. If it is designed specifically to measur
sugar it might be called a 'saccharometer' by th
manufacturer.

Some hydrometers also show potential alcoho
by volume, so that a starting gravity of 104
(known as the 'original gravity' or og) will end wit
approximately 5% alcohol. Without a hydro
meter there is no certain way of knowing that th
fermentation has finished or has stuck. Fu
instructions are usually supplied with eac
instrument.

Recording the original gravity in the log i
important if you intend to repeat that particula
brew.

At 60°F most beer fermentation is finished i
5 to 7 days depending upon the original gravit
and, thereafter, there is no advantage in leaving i
standing in the bin exposed to the unnecessary ris.

'infection. Depending upon the 'body' due to
-sins in suspension beer may not come down
1000.

Temperature for fermenting lager, beer and stout

A maximum-minimum thermometer like the
ne illustrated placed in the coolest spot in the
ouse and left for a minimum of twenty-four
ours will indicate whether you can ferment beer
nd lager successfully. If you have not got a max-
nin type, an ordinary thermometer will do but
ou will have to check it frequently.

Lager
Having produced a good wort for lager you
nnot ferment it with just any yeast at any
mperature. It requires three things—bottom-
rmenting yeast, a non-fluctuating low
rmperature, and time.

Time and temperature are tied together because
l yeast is less active in low temperatures; if the
mperature falls too low, the yeast will stop
orking until it gets warmer. Lager yeast is
pecial in that it operates at the bottom of the wort,
it just naturally keeps to the coolest place. If,
erefore, you cannot find somewhere in the
ouse where a steady temperature around 13°C
55°F) is maintained you cannot make lager. You
ill make a lager-type beer.

Stout
Stout on the other hand requires a much higher
mperature around 18°C (65°F) and a top-
rmenting yeast.

Beer
Beer, whether it be pale ale, mild or bitter,
rments best in a temperature range from 13°C
55°F) to 21°C (70°F).

All fermentations generate some heat and this
alls as the fermentation ceases. The temperature
f fermentation has a big effect upon beer and is
ne of the most difficult things for the home
rewer to control. It can be raised by using a
hermostatic immersion heater, but it cannot be
owered. Having discovered your temperature
ange, endeavour to experiment within it. A lager

cannot be fermented at high temperature an
more than a stout can be fermented at a low on
What you will get is a lager-type or stout-ty
alcoholic drink we call beer.

Carlsberg, Dublin and Burton all becam
famous because of one type of drink in which ea
specialised. You cannot copy them in your ow
kitchen but what you can do as a home brewer
produce your own beer which will be uniqu
Knowing your temperature limitations is a gre
help.

The coolest spot

A hydrometer in a 25 litre fermentation for
check on sg, and a close-up view of a hydromete
This brew was in the darkest corner of the coole
part of a pantry with the objective of producing
lager. When finished it did not compare with t
real thing and was more like a half-lager half-be
than either a beer or a lager, but it was drinkabl

If you can find a place with a low temperature-
a cellar would be ideal—it is worth trying to mal
lager, but you might find the extra days require
for fermentation are not justified by the result.

No-one can give you a precise recipe, metho
and formula for lager without studying yo
conditions at home, so you are on your own, b
there is no need to worry; if your lager is drinkab
you might come to like it and improvement
always possible.

The coolest spot in the house is always the pla
for a barrel whether full of matured beer or empt

How yeast works

To get the best out of yeast you should try t
understand how it works.

Probably one of the most widespread micr
organisms in the world, yeast can live in the so
and, because of its minute size, is airborne. Und
certain conditions it can convert sugar into gas an
alcohol.

It propagates itself by budding; when larg
enough the bud breaks off and goes it alone t
produce its own buds in turn. It must double i
numbers every few hours, otherwise there wou
not be the massive build-up of yeast in th
sediment which is the residue of a fermentation

There are three main sorts of yeast whic
interest home brewers. Top-fermentin
(*saccharomyces cerevisiae*) which rises and is use

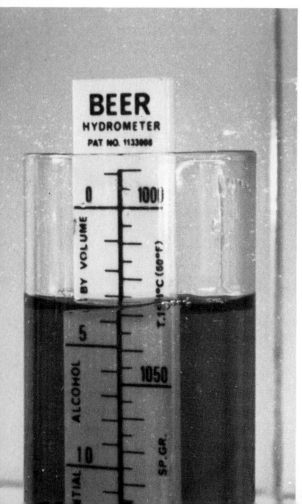

BEER
HYDROMETER
PAT NO. 1133808

r beer and stout; bottom-fermenting *accharomyces carlsbergensis*) which sinks, does ot require air and is used for lager; wild yeast hich drifts about hoping that by chance it will nd in a suitable place where it will be able to feed nd propagate. Wild yeast produces bitter avours, so if you collect some in your brew you ave a liquid not unlike vinegar and you have lost a rew.

Which yeast?

In this picture there are ten different packs of east, some of them from well known old-stablished sources who were supplying yeast efore home brewing became popular, together vith a starter jug and glass measure.

As there is no easy way of recognising yeast on ight, you have to accept the description on the ack in good faith. Obviously, if you have a bad east or, to put it another way, a good brew which ou suspect was spoiled by the yeast, rightly or vrongly you will avoid yeast from that sort of acket ever after.

You have to try different brands because the ype of yeast used will affect the character of your rew. Keep a clear record of how the yeast erforms to your brewing style and always use it resh from the packet.

Yeast bought from a brewery is fine, if you have he nerve to go and ask. Yeast from a bakery will lo the job but its sediment is easily disturbed and t is, therefore, best left for bread-making. Dried ranular baking yeast is usually satisfactory for iome brewing and is worth a trial.

Too much yeast for a quick fermentation is as iad as too little for a slow one. The brewer's ibjective is to strike a good balance; 15g of dried ranular yeast to 25 litres is about right, but might ieed adjusting in the light of experience and lepending upon how the yeast performs.

Pitching the yeast

Dried granular yeast brought to life in the tarter jug shown in the picture above is next •itched into a 10 litre brew with the wort at the ight temperature ready to start fermentation.

Ideally a starter (yeast mixed with wort at '0°F) should be shaken in a bottle with an air)ck. Covering a starter jug containing yeast and vort with a saucer as in the illustration above nd stirring with a spoon involves a calculated

risk, but saves time. Dry granular yeast can b
sprinkled on top of the wort as an alternative t
making a starter, but it takes longer to get going

The fermentation vessel should always have
lid which is only removed when necessary.

The small glass measure shown in the previou
illustration is a useful way of measuring out granu
lar yeast instead of weighing it when you buy it i
large containers.

Occasionally things go wrong and for som
reason the fermentation will not start or it slow
down and stops. On those occasions, assumin
that the sugar content is correct and that you di
pitch some yeast, that the yeast was all right whe
you started and that the temperature has not bee
so high as to kill it, a teaspoon of citric aci
might help. Pitching more yeast is also desirable
Also, giving the brew a good stir may get thing
working again.

Using sediment
for a starter

It is possible to develop the sediment from
bottle of well known beer or stout in a starter fc
your own use so that you have the same yeast as th
professionals. Try it by all means, but have
packet of dried yeast handy in case it does not wor
or it takes too long. Obviously it cannot be done
the brewer has extracted all the sediment.

The other possibility of starting your next bre
with some yeast from the sediment of the last one i
worth trying but if you happen to collect a wil
yeast with a propagation rate faster than the cult
vated yeast, it will outstrip the cultivar and yo
will end up with bad flavours. Try it once or twic
with a small 10 litre brew as an experiment. A
worst, you will lose the brew, and have to sterilis
everything to kill the wild yeast. It might work fc
you and that would be a bonus. The brewin
industry supports both national and internation
research into yeast culture and many hundreds c
cultures have been discovered and propagated. I
is unlikely, therefore, that the amateur will d
better than the professional in his laboratory.

Fortunately, wild yeasts are reputed to be les
tolerant of alcohol than cultivated yeast, so som
of the yeast in the brew will be on your side
Caution is also desirable because beer is suscep
tible to attack by some bacteria tolerant of th
antiseptic properties of hops and alcohol, an
these will spoil the brew if they enter it.

First head removal

Removing surplus yeast and debris carried to the surface by the fermentation. The sides of the container should be wiped to remove the soft yeast adhering to it—a piece of kitchen roll is ideal for the purpose.

Frothy bubbles should appear on the surface of the brew within two days depending to some extent upon the temperature, but a lively yeast pitched in the evening can have a two-inch head the next day.

If the first head is not removed it may give the beer an unpleasant flavour.

It is said that the carpet of bubbles arising from fermenting yeast protects the beer from an invasion of stray wild yeasts and it is better to leave the second head on the beer so that it acts as a protective shield.

It is also true that the removal of the second and third heads does have a favourable influence upon the flavour, so you have scope to experiment and form your own opinion.

Beer which is 'yeast bitten' is not pleasant to drink and it only becomes 'bitten' if the first and second heads are allowed to collapse onto the surface, after which spent yeast cells sink to the bottom and form a sediment.

Second head removal

This picture shows how a second head has formed—in this case within twelve hours—and left a tidemark around the side of this 10 litre fermentation showing its extent before it subsided.

With care this second head can be removed and the tidemark wiped away, when a third head will form providing the brewer with a very interesting and absorbing insight into the behaviour of yeast. The second head can be used to start another brew but to be stored it requires a temperature of °C [37°F].)

From this stage onwards an occasional check with thermometer and hydrometer will enhance your knowledge and allow you to develop your skill in this aspect of brewing.

Keeping the fermentation covered by its own carpet to protect it from stray wild yeast might be a slight over-statement because wild yeast cannot normally perform except in a very low alcohol content, and the gas produced by the fermentation pushing outwards tending to replace and exclude air when the lid is on. There is, however, no substitute for experience so far as the brewer is

concerned and one bad experience is all you nee
to teach you the error of your ways.

If you can maintain the right temperature for
lager fermentation there will be some moveme
on the surface, but head removal is not necessar
Lager can be fermented in a closed container
there is provision for gas to be released through
one-way system such as an air lock.

The smallest measure

A half teaspoon is the smallest piece of equi
ment a home brewer will use. This type of plast
spoon taken from a set of varying measures
useful because, having once established it as bei
the correct size for measuring nutrients, sterili
ing agents, or even yeast, it is easier to use tha
scales and less time consuming. Provided that yo
stick to the same measure all the time, you ca
refer to it in the log in any way you like; it is n
very scientific, but it works.

Brewing timetable

At some stage in home brewing you have
pause and work out a strategy which can be agree
with other members of the family who are likely
be affected. If only an occasional drink is wante
with nothing between brews, there is no problem
However, a continuous supply in bottles or on ta
will require adhering to a plan.

The absolute minimum requirements for
regular daily pint is a 10 litre (2 gallon) fermen
tation bin, a saucepan and 22 bottles. Assuming
6-day maturation period between bottling an
drinking, you need 16 bottles (1 for each pin
brewed) plus 6 more bottles so that the secon
brew can be bottled 6 days before the first bre
runs out, ie a total of 22 bottles.

If, however, you prefer to set aside a regula
evening once a week for brewing or bottling, yo
can adopt a 14-day brewing cycle which will hav
the advantage of giving you 2 extra pints to sha
with your friends in each 14-day period, and wi
allow for breakages. You will need to have 2
bottles to start with.

Once the cycle is running, the first bottle will b
consumed 15 days after brewing and the last bott
28 days after. On the 29th day you will start drink
ing the next brew. Extra bottles will allow longe
maturation; only extra consumption will requi
extra brewing and you already have additional ca
pacity of 2 gallons each week.

14-day brewing cycle:

| | | BOTTLES | | |
		consumed	stock	empty
Day 1	Brew A	–	–	24
Days 2 to 7	Fermentation	–	–	24
Day 8	Bottle A	–	–	8
Days 9 to 14	Maturing	–	16A	8
Day 15	Brew B	1	15A	9
Days 16 to 21	Fermentation	7	8A	16
Day 22	Bottle B	1	7A + 16B	1
Days 23 to 28	Maturing	7	– 16B	8
Day 29	Brew C	1	15B	9
Days 30 to 35	Fermentation	7	8B	16
Day 36	Bottle C	1	7B + 16C	1
Days 37 to 42	Maturing	7	16C –	8
Day 43	Brew D	1	15C	9

continue as from day 16

With a 25 litre (5½ gallons = 44 pints) fermentation bin and the longer maturation period of 14 days you will need 58 pint bottles. The last pint from each brew will therefore be 58 days in the bottle and will be much superior to the first with only 14 days. With this cycle, the plan works out as follows:

Days 1 to 8	Brew, ferment and bottle
Days 9 to 21	Maturing in bottle
Day 22	Bottle 1 ready to drink
Day 44	Begin next brew from day 1
Day 65	Drink last bottle from first brew
Day 66	Start drinking second brew
Day 88	Begin third brew from day 1

This means that you brew roughly every 6 weeks, but during the same period you could brew up at least twice in the 10 litre size using the same bottles as they become empty which will give tremendous scope. The best thing is probably to do both—the large brew for regular pints from a proven brew and the smaller for experimentation. Obviously, if you use barrels rather than bottles, you will need two barrels for a continuous supply.

Ready to bottle

The only sure way of checking if fermentation is finished is by measuring how much sugar is left in the beer. A hydrometer measuring jar is useful but not essential; the one in use in the illustration shows the sugar content as nil in this case, it all having been converted into alcohol.

When the reading is 05 or below it is safe to bottle. The time of bottling is critical in the sense

that gas produced by the secondary fermentation can build up pressure in the bottle and cause a burst, but that also depends upon how much priming sugar you add to the bottle.

A burst is a nuisance for three reasons: you lose the beer and a bottle, you have a mess to clean up, and someone might be injured by broken glass. So care is necessary.

Readings taken daily and recorded in the log will, after a period of time, provide you with a very useful means of analysing your brewing performance. Some beers ferment out more quickly than others. Your log will have details of ingredients, method, time, yeast, temperature, opening gravity, daily fall in gravity, date bottled, result and keeping qualities. From these you can make positive and desirable changes in the ingredients and adjust your brewing performance accordingly.

Bottling

Without a doubt, bottling beer is the worst chore any home brewer has to face.

This picture shows the equipment needed: scale to weigh priming sugar, jug in which to mix it, kitchen roll to soak up the drips, bottles – half pints, pints and flagons, and log, as well as two square metres of working space.

Bottles can be in any combination of sizes; you might consider half pints not worth bothering with but they can be handy on a hot day when a short quick drink is very welcome.

Handling this size of bottling job requires a methodical approach so the first thing the home brewer has to do is ensure he gets the kitchen to himself for a couple of hours, maybe picking a night when the TV programmes are poor and the radio programme is good. The brewer deserves encouragement so a pint of the previous brew can be opened—just to check if it is all right!

If the bottles are thoroughly washed each time after being emptied and the screw cork or a plastic top is used, there is a chance that they will remain sweet. You can test this by smelling each bottle— not an infallible method but it is a short cut. Any sign of an odour means the bottle has to be washed out and sterilised with sodium metabisulphate. An inspection by holding it up to the light will indicate if any other action is required, such as the use of a bottle brush, good old-fashioned elbow grease, or a stain remover which will clean bottles in a few minutes if used with hot water. Stain removers for vacuum flasks, tea and coffee pots and glassware are widely available, and denture stain remover can also be used.

When you first acquire bottles ensure that they are thoroughly clean before use. Take no chances. Having done that once, the easiest way to keep your bottles clean is to keep them full; empty bottles standing on shelves will always be suspect.

After a few sessions the bottles will become familiar, odours identifiable, and your routine easy to follow so that it will not be such a bad chore after all. At worst it occurs every other week.

Priming for secondary fermentation

In theory if fermentation takes place inside a closed container such as a beer bottle, one of three things will happen. The gas produced will build up to such a pressure as to burst the bottle or blow the cork, and the beer will be lost. Or the yeast will become inhibited and stop producing alcohol and gas, but only after maximum pressure on the yeast and bottle has been achieved. When the bottle is opened the contents will erupt in foam, bubbles and sediment and some of the contents will be lost. There might be a mess to clean up, some clothes sent to the cleaners and at worst a redecoration job on the wall, usually at about picture rail height. Or thirdly, the fermentation will have stopped because the supply of nutrients, mainly sugar, has been exhausted by the yeast and when opened the beer will pour easily and the restricted gas will gently escape by rising to the surface in a continuous stream of small bubbles.

The objective of the home brewer is to achieve the last of these behaviours and this can be done in five ways, the first three of which are illustrated.

1 Add half a small teaspoon of sugar to each bottle. It is best to start with less than half a spoonful and gradually increase the amount with experience until you achieve the perfect result.

2 The second is more accurate. Weigh out the required amount of sugar, 6g to 1 litre (1oz to 1 gallon) but not more, mix it with sufficient beer to prime all the bottles and then dose each one with the same quantity. The picture shows a small calibrated measure being used.

3 Mix the sugar and beer as above and dose each bottle from a spirit measure which can be obtained in various sizes. This is a quick and very accurate way of obtaining consistency, but chrome-plated

measures are not intended for use with beer so have to be thoroughly rinsed and dried immediately after use.

4 Bottle before the fermentation ceases and the sg is below 1008, but do not add sugar. The reading 1008 is a rather arbitrary figure and may be too high for you, so experiment by starting at 1005.

5 Mix sugar and beer together and add it to a second container into which you run-off the beer after it has finished fermenting and started to clear. You then bottle from the second container which, if fitted with a tap, makes the bottling job so much easier. It also guarantees a consistent secondary fermentation throughout the brew, but only if you have the same amount of beer in each bottle (see upper illustration on page 38).

Ordinary sugar is suitable for use in priming. Invert sugar induces the secondary fermentation more quickly but it is not really worth the extra cost for the time saved. To say the least, getting the priming right for the secondary fermentation is tricky and requires care. If the amount of air space in the bottle varies the performance of the beer will also be variable. Aim for about two inches of air space at all times.

Siphoning

Plastic tube of about 10mm diameter is suitable for siphoning beer from the fermenting bin. Smaller diameter may become frustrating by being too slow for beer, especially when you have fifty bottles to fill from a 25 litre (5½ gallon) brew.

It should be attached firmly to the bin so that it will not stir up the sediment whilst in use. There will be some sediment anyway, but keep it to the minimum or it will take longer for the beer to fall clear in the bottle.

A piece of string or nylon cord can be used to hold the siphon tube rigid. Tie five knots in the doubled cord, one at the end and four at intervals, so that the tube can be pushed through and be adjusted for height in the bin. It has to be a fairly tight fit. It is held in position by ordinary spring clothes pegs which are fastened to the bin on opposite sides. The illustration makes it clear.

You may be able to design something better depending upon the shape of the container lip, like bending stainless steel wire to slip onto its edge as illustrated on page 37.

The advantage of these two systems is that they are simple and with experience you can adjust the siphon tube to keep it above the sediment. The

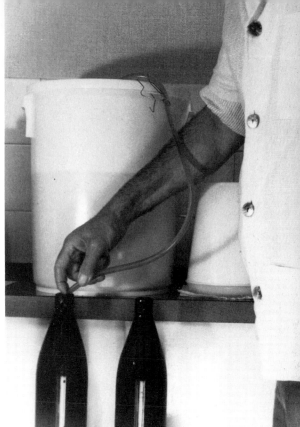

chances of a breakage with a glass U-shaped
siphon tube are eliminated.

Initial surge

Once a flow has been induced in the tube, liquid
will transfer itself through a higher level to a lower
level without further bother. To start the flow,
there is no easier way than sucking out the air yourself. A siphon with a hand pump is available but it
hardly seems worth the expense.

The initial flow will be a surge and it is best to
start by using either a large jug or litre or quart
bottles. As it slows down, smaller bottles can be
filled direct from the siphon.

To stop the flow whilst transferring from bottle
to bottle just close the end of the tube with your
finger as shown in the illustration. Of course, it is
essential that your hands are thoroughly clean
before starting.

Transferring containers

Under normal circumstances beer will clear by itself without any help from the brewer by the addition of finings. When the fermentation has stopped an inspection will indicate that the beer near the surface is clear. At that stage it might be convenient to draw off the clear beer into another container as a stage in assisting the clearance of the remainder. The illustration shows this being done. If the beer is intended for a barrel, isinglass or gelatine finings should be added at this stage to help clarification which takes a long time in a barrel compared with the short time in a bottle.

Corks and bottles

There are three types of bottle and four types of closure in use by home brewers. All are illustrated here.

The easiest are the screw corks with a rubber band. No longer in use commercially and difficult to collect, these bottles can still be found and publicans are sometimes pleased to let them go for the price of a drink. Metal screw tops are also easy to use and spares can be bought at any store catering for the home brewer. The tops have a useful life of several brews and should be discarded once damaged. The perfectionist will use new for each brew but that is not necessary.

Metal crown corks as used by the trade are excellent.

Plastic crown corks or bottle stoppers can be dangerous should they stick and cause pressure to build up in the bottle, when they will fly off at high

velocity. It is best not to prime bottles with plastic tops to avoid a build-up of pressure from a secondary fermentation. The beer will be draught type and not as lively as ordinary bottled beer, but nevertheless it will be very drinkable and should be tried as an experiment. The plastic closures can be used more than once which makes them economical. If warmed in hot water they become supple and will go over the lip of the bottle easily. Plastic caps are also useful to cover empty bottles which usually have metal corks when full.

Bottles for crown corks can be bought in new condition.

When glass fractures it sometimes flies apart or just cracks. Beer bottles are made to withstand considerable pressure and if they fracture they usually, but not always, crack.

Sterilising

Swilling out the solution of sodium metabisulphate in which screw corks were sterilised. It is always desirable to ensure that screw corks and rubbers and plastic stoppers are absolutely clean before re-use.

Fastening the tops

Crown corks can be very easily fitted with the two-handled tool illustrated. Alternatively, one clout with a heavy mallet or hammer is sufficient to secure them using the small hand tool shown although considerable practice is necessary to get it right.

Avoiding sediment in the barrel

A brew which was transferred from a 25 litre fermentation bin to a smaller container several days previously being casked.

About 150g (5oz) of sugar dissolved in some of the beer was placed in the barrel first to prime it, and about three quarters of the brew has been run off through a siphon which was very carefully placed with the inlet well above the sediment.

Having completed that operation, there is no point in replacing the siphon when what remains of the brew can be run off through the tap and the bin gently tilted to leave the sediment behind, particularly if it is clear enough to see the bottom which it should be if finings were added when it was transferred.

A short cut would be to run it all through the tap, but there is a risk of picking up an infection from our old enemy the wild yeast because of the greater exposure of the beer to air.

Knowing the risks always helps with a highly vulnerable organic substance like beer; there is no substitute for the knowledge and skill gained by experience and practice. At this level of home brewing, it would seem a waste of energy, time, enthusiasm, materials, effort, skill and money to get it wrong and not have any suitable beer to drink.

In store

A store (overleaf) of 110 pints of beer contained in 72 bottles and a small barrel holding 19 pints.

Good quality beer in bottles will keep indefinitely and be better for keeping. There is more than enough here for a fairly hectic New Year's Eve party at home, and with a few regular visitors it will soon go.

Using labels to identify the brew is a little

41

ostentatious for beer. Paper labels soon deteriorate as they almost inevitably get wet.

A good way to identify the brew is by use of markers on each row or between each brew. Different colours of crown cork and little self-adhesive coloured stickers are available, and the colour used can be recorded in the log. An alternative is to buy small self-adhesive labels and number them, or self-adhesive labels already numbered. There is no need to label every bottle.

Maturation in barrels

Covering a full five-gallon barrel with a large heavy-grade polythene bag before placing it in a cupboard in the garage to mature. The plastic bag keeps the outside of the barrel clean and does not affect the beer.

A five-gallon barrel will take some time to clear and come into prime condition, much longer than bottled beer, and whilst you can manage without fining bottled beer you have time against you with a barrel. It takes much too long to clear, so fining it is essential.

If it is fitted with a carbon dioxide injector as the one illustrated, it can be charged and then put out of the way for two or three weeks.

A full barrel of mature beer is probably the peak for the home brewer. The only area where he can make a further advance is to acquire a wood cask, but that requires more specialised knowledge and is much more trouble to sterilise. Suffice to say that keeping a plastic barrel clean and the beer in it wholesome is a much easier task.

The major problem in keeping barrels clean is the difficulty in getting them under a tap for the water to swish around and to remove cleansing and sterilising fluids before refilling. You have to be absolutely certain that they are absolutely clean, otherwise your efforts are wasted.

Barrels are available with large or small openings: both are illustrated in this book. Both have advantages and disadvantages. With the small opening it is easier to get a good airtight seal and hold the pressure, with or without an injector. The large opening has more risks in being airtight because of the larger area, but it is easier to inspect and clean. Anyone who has had experience in maintaining air pressure will know some of the problems even when using plastic connections.

When buying a new barrel try it out first with water. If the opening leaks take it to be replaced because it will never be airtight. Some barrels are guaranteed by the manufacturers. There is n

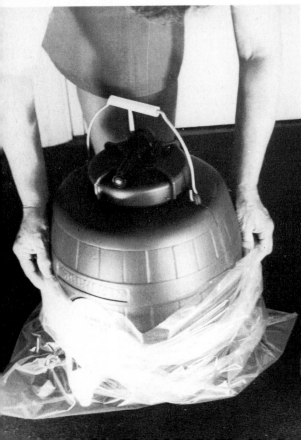

point in having a CO$_2$ injector on a barrel which is not airtight.

Spheres and cubes not illustrated are available for home brewers. They have an advantage in being white transparent plastic so the brewer can see the level of the contents.

Barrels, spheres and cubes

If, ignoring all aspects of beer in bottles, you decide to dispense your beer from barrels or other containers known as spheres or cubes which come in various sizes up to 25 litres, you must have at least two. These need not be the same size and the illustration shows a reasonable combination.

The large fermentation bin will cope with the large barrel; the small bucket is just about right for the small barrel. The small sizes are not too big for experimental brews (when you first start home brewing all brews are experimental) whereas the large size might be.

Small barrels also have other advantages. The one in the illustration has travelled many thousands of miles to all sorts of remote spots in the hills of Wales and the moors of Scotland filled with clear prime beer either from the large barrel or flagons and will keep four people going very well for two or three days.

If you are definitely keeping to barrels you will need a fifth container to rack beer into prior to casking. The size will be determined by the requirements of your personal brewery.

Visual test for clarity

An sg measuring jar being used for a visual test. In this case the beer was put into the jar and sealed with a transparent jam-pot cover at the same time as the beer was run off into a barrel. The beer had been racked off its yeast sediment when the sg was 1010 and then two days later was run off into a barrel.

The purpose here is to watch the beer fall clear in the measuring jar as an alternative to checking the barrel which is stored elsewhere and should not be disturbed. You need a space where the measuring jar can stand undisturbed. It can be part of a home brewer's education to watch it clear, but good beer is produced purely on a time basis which you learn from experience.

Small bottles will fall clear quicker than large ones; a barrel requires patience and a little more time. The visual aspect of this exercise helps to pass the time fruitfully.

Sediment

By the natural order of things a fermentation will automatically produce a sediment which will have 'off' flavours from the spent yeast and minute solid matter which falls out of suspension. Sediment does not improve the beer or the digestion.

So how to avoid sediment? Very carefully pour from the bottle into a glass jug and then serve from the jug into glasses.

Be courteous to your guests by serving your beer in glassware so that both you and they can see the clarity, the bubbles and the 'head'. If you do not use glass the amount of beer in the jug will be invisible beneath the head formed by bubbles (this is particularly important when drawing from a barrel).

There is no way to avoid a sediment where there has been a secondary fermentation in a bottle, a barrel or a sphere. All you can do with a bottle is very carefully and slowly pour until the sediment floats along to the neck and then stop, leaving the dregs behind. Once you stop pouring and tip the bottle back, the sediment will swirl into the beer.

When drawing from a barrel the sediment, once it has settled, will be no problem until the last few pints are reached, providing the barrel does not get disturbed.

Putting clear carbonated beer into bottles and barrels is outside the scope of a home brewer. The nearest you can get is to allow the beer to fall clear after fermentation, apply some gelatine or isinglass finings to take all the yeast down to the bottom and then rack the beer into another container, be it a barrel, sphere, or cube.

If you fit an injector it will help to keep the beer in good condition and avoid air entering the barrel to replace beer drawn off. Full instructions come with the injector and there are several to choose from. The main problem is to keep the mouth of the container airtight.

If you are not worried about the sediment or if you cannot get the beer to fall clear but it tastes all right, you can use pottery or metal tankards. What could be better than drinking your home-brewed beer from an antique pewter tankard? Nowadays genuine high-class bottled beer still comes with a slight sediment, but it is rare and difficult to find.

You will get as much pleasure from brewing our own beer as from drinking it and, with xperience, will produce a brew to be proud of.

Basic recipe tables

The following table for brewing 25 litres (5½ allons) of beer indicates the ingredients for pro-ucing beer graded from very light lager-type to eavy stout-type. A variation in any of the ingre-ients, or the weight used will make a noticeable ifference to the beer. The brewer can, therefore, nake his own adjustments. Plain wheat and barley rain can be used in any brew to add fullness and lavour but are no substitute for malted barley.

All quantities are given in grammes; approxi-ate imperial equivalents are given below, which re accurate enough for home brewing and spring-alance domestic scales.

15g	½oz	340g	¾lb
30g	1oz	454g	1lb
55g	2oz	500g	1·1lb
85g	3oz	900g	2lb
115g	4oz	1000g	2·2lb
226g	½lb	(1kg)	

	Lager	Light Ale		Pale Ale		Mild		Bitter		Old Ale		Stout		
Hops (choice marked +)	70–90	70–100		80–110		90–120		100–130		100–130		100–130		Singly or in combination
Hallertau and Saaz	+													
Styrian Goldings	+	+		+				+						
Goldings (all types)		+		+				+						
Northern Brewer				+		+		+		+		+		
Bramling Cross				+		+		+		+		+		
Fuggles						+		+		+		+		
Bullion								+		+		+		
Barley	+	+		+		+		+		+		+		
Wheat	+	+		+		+		+		+		+		
Light powdered malt	900	900		900		900		900		900	226	226		Choice
Dark powdered malt				15	15	115				226		900	226	
Light malt syrup			900		900				900					
Dark malt syrup							900				900		900	
Light crystal malt	226	340		454		454		680		680		680		For flavour and strength
Dark crystal malt						30				55		115		
Flaked maize		15		15		55		55		55		85		
Flaked oats										70		115		
Torrified barley	15	15		15		55		55		55		85		
Plain sugar	680	1000		1000		1000		1000		1000		1090		
Demerara sugar		226		340		500		500		500		500		
Glucose chips								115		226		340		

Supplies and equipment

Some of the following companies issue a price list and catalogue and supply by direct mail order. Some of them only supply through retail outlets which are located widely throughout the country.

The Boots Company Ltd, Nottingham.

Brewitt Home Brew Centres Ltd, 57 St John's Road, Liverpool.

CWE Ltd, Cawston, Norfolk.

EDME Ltd, Mistley, Manningtree, Essex.

Leigh Williams & Sons, Tattenhall, nr Chester.

W.R. Loftus (Retail) Ltd, 1–3 Charlotte Street, London.

Ritchie Products, Rolleston Road, Burton-on-Trent.

Rogers (Meade) Ltd, Broseley, Salop.

Savory & Moore Ltd, 177 Preston Road, Brighton.

Southampton Homebrews Ltd, 12 Rochester Street, Northam, Southampton.

Unican Foods Limited, Bath Road, Bristol.

Vinaide Brewing & Food Products, 28 Swan Street, Manchester 4.

Further reading

The following books will be of interest to the home brewer.

Berry, C.J.J. *Home Brewed Beers and Stouts*. The Amateur Winemaker, 1963

Boston, R. *Beer and Skittles*. Collins, 1976

Carr, J.G. *Biological Principles in Fermentation*. Heinemann, 1968

Corran, H.S. *A History of Brewing*. David & Charles, 1975

Duddington, C.L. *Plain Man's Guide to Beer*. Pelham, 1974

Foster, T. *Doctor Foster's Book of Beer*. Adam and Charles Black, 1979

Line, D. *The Big Book of Brewing*. The Amateur Winemaker, 1974

Newsom, W.G. *The Happy Brewer*. The Amateur Winemaker, 1978

Shales, K. *Advanced Home Brewing*. The Amateur Winemaker, 1972

Tayleur, W.H.T. *Home Brewing & Wine Making*. Penguin, 1973

Turner, B. *The Beermaker's Companion*. Granada, 1980

Turner, B.C.A. & Moon, D.J. *Simple Guide to Homemade Beer*. Mills & Boon, 1968

Watney, J. *Beer is Best*. Peter Owen, 1974

Index